The Kray's Book Of Slang

By Steve and Rebecca Wraith

JOHN DILLENGER WAS THE N°1
BANK ROBBER OF ALL TIME

[signature]

[signature]

Ralwin

mediaarts

Published in 2019 by Media Arts

Copyright © 2019 Steve and Rebecca Wraith
All rights reserved

The moral rights of the authors have been asserted

British Library Cataloguing in Publication Data:
A catalogue record for this book is available from
the British Library

ISBN-13:
978-0-9927023-2-8

Cover design
David Stanyer

Layout
Neil Jackson, Media Arts
www.media-arts.co.uk

Printed & bound by Books Factory
Proudly published Up North

Foreword By Freddie Foreman

I remember Reggie Kray bringing out his 'Slang' book and the publicity surrounding it. Former criminals writing books wasn't really something anybody had considered until then.
That book was followed by the Twins autobiography in the nineties and since then books about the Krays have just kept on coming.
I've written a few books over the years myself and have been mentioned in many others. My latest book 'Freddie Foreman's Final Photo Album' has been well received and brought back a lot of happy memories.

Slang is part of our culture in London. It has changed a lot over the years but most of it remains the same.
Looking through the unseen photos of the twins and the Kray family brings back a lot of memories. Some good and some best forgotten.
This photo at Ronnie Krays funeral shows myself alongside Steve Wraith with Reggie and Charlie Kray. This was the day I first met Steve.
Our friendship has lasted since that sad day in 1995.
I want to wish my good friend Steve and his beautiful daughter Rebecca the very best of luck with this book, I am sure it will be very successful.

Freddie Foreman
July 2019.

Foreword By Charles Salvador

It's absolutely brilliant Steve and Rebecca are doing a tribute book on the Twins.
Let's face it the Krays will never die. And why should they?
They was loved and respected by many.
It was in Parkhurst Jail I first met them back in 1975. When men were real men.
Fearless. Strong willed and loyal!
It's no secret Ronnie was the best pal I ever had and for 20 years he remained a
true loyal pal of mine.
We even ended up in the mad house together. 'Broadmoor Asylum'.
Crazy times but wonderful memories. It's all in my book 'The Krays And Me.'

Do I miss them? Too much. It's not the same no more. But memories live on.
Stories become legendary. The Kray Twins are forever in the criminal history
files. But always remember this and remember I said it.
They were real men of honour.
And not one day of their punishment did they ever cry.

Charles Salvador
July 2019.

Foreword By Rod Harrison

When Steve contacted me and requested I sort a forward out with Charlie for his new book I obviously said 'Will do! What's the book about?'
He replied 'the Krays' and I thought 'for fuck sake what is left to say with there already being over 50 books written on the Twins?'
But when he explained it was a 30th anniversary edition of Regs Book of slang I thought it could be an interesting project and when Steve said he was doing with his daughter Rebecca I thought 'nice one. Young blood, young ideas' so I wish you all the best Rebecca on your first book.
Do it your way and I am sure it will be a successful project .You've already read Charlie's foreword but he insisted I had to do a post script as well!

Well, after racking my brain to say some thing nice about Mr Wraith here it is !!
Sorry Steve .
I first heard the name Steve Wraith connected to the twins early 90s when Steve went in business with Reg on the tee shirts and other Kray merchandise which led Steve to go on and meet Reg. A meeting with Ron followed this and he went onto be involved in various ventures with the twins mainly through Reg, who was always the business man and with Charlie Kray, who was always up for making a few quid (sometimes upsetting Reg in the process!)
I first saw Steve as a young man at several charity events held up and down the country to highlight the Twins situation and help make a few quid for charity.
They were great nights but we never really got to know each other properly then as I was more than 25 years older than him so we moved in different circles.
But I did get to know him later on and we seemed to hit it off.
Now I consider him a pal.
So with Steve's association with all three brothers and his endless phone calls from Reg at all hours with instructions to send this guy a watch, see this geezer about business etc etc Steve is the ideal man to do this anniversary book with his daughter.
Good luck pal and thanks for your continued support for Charlie in our bid to get him the progression he deserves.

Respect

Rod Harrison
July 2019.

Introduction By Steve and Rebecca Wraith

Steve Wraith
Born: 16th February 1972
Convictions: None
Age: 47
Hobbies: Writing.
Ambitions: To be recognised as an author and actor and to provide for my family.

In 1989 Reggie Kray released 'Book Of Slang' to an unsuspecting public. The book was A5 in size and 64 pages long. Priced at £4.99 it was released by publishers Sidgwick and Jackson Ltd from London. The book contained a foreword from his close friend Patsy Manning and some previously unpublished photographs of Reggie Kray and his twin brother Ronnie who had ruled the East End criminal fraternity for the best part of the 1960's before their arrest in 1968.

The book was a simple format and introduced the reader to 'Cockney' slang, American slang and 'Criminal' slang, and there was also a little taste of Reggie and Patsy's poetry thrown in for good measure at the end.
Reggie opened the book with an explanation of why he had decided to put pen to paper after a failed suicide attempt in Long Lartin Prison. He had experienced an extreme case of paranoia and claimed he had been 'spiked' by a fellow inmate who placed a drug in a curry he had eaten. Reggie cut his wrists with the glass from his shattered spectacles but was found by prison officers who stemmed the blood flow and saved his life. He was transferred to Parkhurst Prison Hospital where he had time to reflect on his mental state and do a lot of self analysis. He goes onto explain that as he writes the book he is in a better mental state and that he holds no grudges against the Police that arrested him or the judge that sentenced him. All he really craved at that time was a light at the end of the tunnel. He was hoping to be de-categorised from Cat A and take his first step on the road to eventual parole and freedom. Sadly this hope was only realised when he had days left to live.

I decided to release this book for a few reasons. Firstly it is 30 years since Reg released his own book of Slang. In that time both Reg and Patsy have passed away and I thought it would be a nice way to pay tribute to them and their achievement. In that 30 year period there has been an increase in slang words that have been adopted in the UK and my 12 year old daughter Rebecca has selected the ones you can read within these pages. As a 'kray' collector I have bought many interesting items including family photographs. Inside this book you will find over 40 unseen photographs of Ronnie, Reggie and Charlie Kray and some of their close friends and family. Releasing this book has given me the chance to share those photographs with you.

As in the first book there is some poetry to close with. The poems are by Reggie and Ronnie Kray and me. The poems were previously published in a limited edition book that I released a few years ago so many of you will not have had the pleasure of reading them.

Finally I wanted my daughter to learn a valuable lesson in helping me with this book. That to earn money you have to work for it. She has embraced that opportunity and I have paid her for her time. She is also on a cut of the profits! The Twins would be proud of her negotiating skills!

I hope you get as much pleasure out of reading this book and looking at the new photographs as we did making it.

Steve Wraith
July 2019.

Rebecca Wraith
Born: 6th November 2006
Age: 12
Hobbies: Social media addict.
Ambitions: To be a socialite and social media influencer.

My Dad, Steve Wraith, asked me to help him with a book he was writing. The book was about Cockney Rhyming Slang. I agreed to help him write out the book. I started researching the slang words on the internet and started typing the book in April. I finished in August 2019. I completed my task with the help of my friend Georgia Dial. To conclude my task means a lot to me, as I get to make some money. When I first started writing the book for my Dad, I was very slow, and did not do much in the first 2 months. Now I have finished the book, it has made me realise that it takes hard work to earn money, and that it doesn't just grow on trees. I hope you enjoy the book.

Rebecca Wraith Aged 12
July 2019.

Aa :

Alan Whickers - Knickers
Alexander Hleb - Pleb
Albert Halls - Balls
Ali G - Pee
Ali McGraw - Score
All Time Loser - Boozer
All Night Rave - Shave
Alan Ladd - Bad
Alan Knott - Hot
Alan Border - Out Of Order
A la Mode - Code
Adam And Eve - Believe
Adam And The Ants - Pants
Air Gunner - Stunner
Al Capone - Telephone

Ronnie Kray being driven in an MG by a friend.

Bb :

Bacon Baps - Flaps
Bacon And Eggs - Legs
Bacon Rind - Mind
Bag For Life - Wife
Babe Ruth - Truth
Baked Bean - Queen
Baa Lamb - Tram
Bacardi Breezer - Freezer
Babbling Brook - Crook
Bacon Bonce - Nonce
Bag Of Fruit - Suit
Bag Of Yeast - Beast
Bale Of Straw - Raw
Baked Potato - See You Later
Bag Of Sand - 1000 Pound

Charlie Kray Snr. and Violet Kray in a bedroom at Cedra Court.

Cc :

Cabin Cruiser - Boozer
Cadbury's Snack - Back
Calvin Klein - Wine/Fine
Camel's Hump - Dump
Canterbury Tales - Wales
Captain Kirk - Work
Smash And Grab - Cab
Captain Cook - Look
Candle Wax - Tax
Cape Of Good Hope - Soap
Cane And Able - Table
Canary Wharf - Dwarf

Frances Kray with an unknown friend in the yard at Vallance Road.

Dd :

Daily Mail - Tale
Derby Kelly - Belly
Deep Sea Diver - Fiver
Dinky doo - Twenty-Two
Donald Duck - Luck
Do Me Good - Wood
Dog And Bone - Telephone
Dicky Bird - Word
Door To Door - Four
Dixie Deans - Jeans
Dot And Dash - Moustache
Daft And Barny - Army
Down The Drains - Brains
Dribs And Drabs - Crabs
Duke Of Kent - Rent

Aunt May at the door on Vallance Road.

Ee :

Earwig - Twig
East And West - Vest
Elsie Tanner - Spanner
Early Doors - Pair Of Drawers
Easter Bunny - Funny
Easy Rider - Cider
Eddie Grundies - Undies
Eiffel Tower - Shower
Eighteen Pence - Sense
Elephant Trunk - Drunk
Elastic Bands - Hands
Eggs And Kippers - Slippers
Egg Yoke - Joke
Early Hours - Flowers
Eddy Grant - Plant

Violet Kray with Limehouse Willy and his wife.

Ff :

False Start - Fart
Feather And Flip - Kip
Fat Boy Slim - Gym
Field Of Wheat - Street
Fish Hook - Book
Frog And Toad - Road
Fairy Snuff - Stuff
Fanny Craddock - Haddock
Far East - Priest
Four By Two - Jew
Fork And Knife - Wife
Finger And Thumb - Rum
Fine And Dandy - Brandy
Flowery Dell - Cell
Fly-By-Nights - Tights

Ronnie Kray sparring in the yard at Vallance Road with
Tommy 'The Bear' Brown.

Gg :

Ginger Beer - Engineer
Gooseberry Tart - Cart
Gregory Peck - Neck
Gypsy's Kiss - Miss
Garden Gate - Mate
Grass In The Park - Nark
Gates Of Rome - Home
Gary Ablett - Tablet
George Raft - Draft
Grey Mare - Fare
German Band - Hand
Geoff Hurst - Thirst
Gay And Frisky - Whisky
Glasgow Ranger - Stranger
Giraffe - Laugh

Gary Kray with Violet and an unknown friend.

Hh :

Half Inch - Pinch
Ham Shank - Yanks
Heap Of Coke - Bloke
Hearts Of Oak - Broke
Harry Wagg - Fag
Harry Tate - State
Harpers And Queens - Jeans
Hedge And Ditch - Pitch
Henry Moore - Door
Herring And Kipper - Stripper
Highland Fling - Ring
How Do You Do - Shoe
Hot Cross Bun - Nun
Holy Friar - Liar
Holy Ghost - Toast

Violet Kray with friends, Shiela and Dot.

Ii :

Iron Horse - Toss
I Suppose - Nose
Irish Rose - Nose
Iron Tank - Bank
Irish Jig - Wig
Isle Of Wight - Light
Ivory Band - Hand
Afloat - Overcoat
Ice Cream Freezer - Geezer
In And Out - Gout
In The Nude - Food
Insects And Ants - Underpants
Inky Smudge - Judge
Itch And Scratch - Match
Isle Of White - Right

Ronnie Kray asleep in a chair with his dog Mr. Bill on his lap at Vallance Road.

Jj :

Jimmy Riddle - Piddle
Jah Rule - School
Jam Jar - Car
Joe Baxi - Taxi
Joe Blake - Steak
Joe Rook - Crook
Jumping Jack - Back
Jam Tarts - Heart
Joe Brown - Town
Jim Skinner - Dinner
Jack And Jill - Bill
Jenny Lee - Key
Johnny Horner - Corner
Jack Jones - Owns
Jack Tar - Bar

Bare chested Charlie Kray on his release from prison at
George and Sue Dwyer's.

Kk :

Kerry Packered - Knackered
Ken Smee - Pee
King Death - Breath
Kate Karney - Army
Ken Dodd - Wad
Kippers - Slippers
King Lears - Ears
Kidney Punch - Lunch
Kettle On The Hob - Fob
Khyber Pass - Glass
Kilkenny - Penny
Kate Moss-ed - Lost
Kick And Prance - Dance
Kate And Sydney - Stake And Kidney

Charlie Kray Snr and Violet at Steeple Bay.

Ll :

Lady Godiva - Fiver
Laugh And Titter - Bitter
Lemon Squeezy - Easy
Lemon Squeezer - Geezer
Left In The Lurch - Church
Lemonade - Spade
Leo Sayer - All-Dayer
Light And Dark - Park
Lilley And Skinner - Dinner
Lillian Gish - Fish
Linen Draper - Newspaper
Lions Lair - Chair
Loaf Of Bread - Head
Loop The Loop - Soup
Lollipop - Shop

Violet Kray on holiday at Steeple Bay.

Mm :

Mae West - Best
Major Loda - Soda
Moby Dick - Sick
Micro Chip - Nip
Mutt And Jeff - Deaf
Mince Pies - Eyes
Me And You - Menu
Marbles And Conkers - Bonkers
Macaroni - Pony
Major Stevens - Evens
Mangle And Wringer - Singer
Mickey Mouse - Scouse
Merryheart - Tart
Mum And Dad - Mad
Mystic Megs - Legs

Reggie Kray at Steeple Bay.

Nn :

Nutmegs - Legs
Ned Kelly - Telly
Nanny Goat - Coat
Near And Far - Bar
Nelson Eddys - Readies
Nanny Goat - Boat
Nuclear Sub - Pub
Nobby Stiles - Piles
Needle And Pin - Gin
Nuremberg Trials - Piles
Nails And Tacks - Fax
Newington Butts - Guts
North And South - Mouth
Nelson Mandelas - Stellas
Nervo And Knox - Fox

Ronnie Kray aged around 20 in the sea.

Oo :

Obadiah - Fire
Ocean Pearl - Girl
Ocean Wave - Shave
Oedipus Rex - Sex
Oily Rag - Fag
Oliver Twist - Fist
On The Floor - Poor
Once A Week - Cheek
One And The Other - Brother
One Time Looker - Hooker
Ones And Twos - Shoes
Oscar Asche - Cash
Oxford Schollar - Dollar
Oxo Cube - Tube
Frank Bough - Off

Ronnie Kray at the caravan at Steeple Bay.

Pp :

Pete Tong - Wrong
Peas In The Pot - Hot
Paraffin Lamp - Tramp
Peter Pan - Can
Pigs Ear - Beer
Pat And Mick - Sick
Pen And Ink - Stink
Pig And Roast - Toast
Pimple And Blotch - Gotch
Pleasure And Pain - Rain
Pick And Mix - Sticks
Penny Come Quick - A Trick
Pipe Your Eye - Cry
Pots And Dishes - Wishes
Pinky And Perky - Turkey

Charlie Kray Snr and Violet Kray on holiday.

Qq :

Quaker Oat - Coat
Queen Mum - Bum
Queens Park Ranger - Stranger
Quentin Crisp - Lisp
Quack - Doctor
Queenie - Mother Or Wife
QE - Going Queen's Evidence

'Mad' Teddy Smith and Ronnie Kray at the caravan at Steeple Bay.

Rr :

Rabbit And Pork - Talk
Radio Ones - Runs
Radio Rental - Mental
Rag And Bone - Throne
Rags And Riches - Breeches
Raspberry Ripple - Cripple
Raspberry Ripple - Nipple
Raspberry Tart - Heart
Rat And Mouse - House
Rats And Mice - Dice
Razor - Blazer
Read And Write - Bite
Reels Of Cotton - Rotten
Rubarb Pill - Hill
Rhythm And Blues - Shoes

Frances and Reggie Kray with Tommy 'The Bear' Brown at Steeple Bay.
The photo was taken on June 9th 1963.

Ss :

Salmon And Trout - Snout
Salmon And Trout - Stout
San Toy - Boy
Santas Grotto - Blotto
Saucepan Handle - Candle
Saucepan Lid - Quid
Sausage And Mash - Crash
Scapa Flow - Go
Scoobie Doo - Clue
Scotch Peg - Egg
Scotch Pegs - Legs
Selina Scott - Spot

Frances Kray at the caravan at Steeple Bay with her dog Mitsy.

Tt :

Tartan Banner - Tanner
Tea Leaf - Thief
Tea, Two And A Bloater - Motor
Teapot Lid - Kid
These And Those - Toes
This And That - Cat
Thomas Tilling - Shilling
Tick Tock - Clock
Tiddly Wink - Drink
Tin Bath - Laugh
Tin Of Fruit - Suit
Tin Tack - Sack
Tin Tank - Bank
Tina Turner - Earner

Frances with Mitsy and Tommy 'The Bear' Brown at Steeple Bay.

Uu :

Uncle Bert - Shirt
Uncle Fred - Bread
Uncle Ned - Head
Uncle Ted - Bed
Uncle Wilth - Filth
Uncle Willy - Silly
Uncle Ben - Ten
Uncle Billy - Chilly
Uncle Bob - Job
Uncle Fester - Child Molester
Uncle Gus - Bus
Uncle Reg - Veg
Uncle Toby - Moby
Uncle And Aunts - Plants
Union Jack - Black

Charlie Kray on holiday.

Vv :

Vera Lynn - Gin
Vera Lynns - Skins
Vauxhall Novas - Jehovas
Vera Lynn - Chin
Veronica Lake - Break
Vicar's Daughter - Quarter
Vincent Price - Ice
Vincent Van Gogh - Cough
Virginia Wades - Shades

A young Frances Kray at Steeple Bay.

Ww :

Wallace And Grommit - Vomit
Weasle And Stoat - Coat
Weavers Chair - Prayer
Weeping Willow - Pillow
West Ham Reserves - Nerves
Westminister Abbey - Shabby
Whale And Gail - Out Of Jail
Whistle And Flute - Suit
White Mice - Ice
Wilkie Bard - Warrent Card
Widdow Twanky - Hanky
Winona Ryder - Cider
Wobbly Jelly - Telly
Wooden Plank - Yank

Reggie Kray on the beach.

Xx :

X Division - Swindlers, Thieves
X's hall - The Sessions House
X-Ray - A 10,000 Dollar Bill

Reggie Kray in Spain.

Yy :

You And Me - Tea
You Must - Crust
Yarmouth Bloater - Motor
Yogi Bear - Hair
Yoyo Ma - Car
Yul Brynner - Dinner
Yuri Geller - Steller

Violet Kray taken by surprise at home!

Zz :

Zig And Zag - Shag
Zachary Scotts - Trots
Zippy And Bungle - Jungle

Ronnie Kray horseriding.

Perchance We Met

Perchance we met
Our life together was set
It all changed the day we met
I'll always remember that day
You affect me that way
It's the little things you say

We were on the same wavelength
And meeting you
Has given my life joy and strength
I first saw you at a glance
It was meant to through by chance.

Frances Kray on honeymoon in Athens.

Rapture

As she walked the back of her hair jumped
Which made my heart beat
And made me want to tap my feet
It was also the way she walked
And the special way she talked
She makes my heart go thump, thump
Each time I see her hair jump
I'm in bliss each time we kiss
The rapture of her lips are heavenly bliss
When we cuddle
My heart goes boomp, boomp
And misses a beat
I'm all in a muddle
In rapture and bliss.

Frances Kray at Heathrow Airport.

A Friend

Jon Bon Jovi is a friend to the end
It's his nature
It's his feature
A friend he really values
This is one of his strangest traits
He figures a friend is above all misery and hates

To Jon a friend is the ultimate jewel
Some mainly to be valued above all
Some mainly that he knows to be life's jewel for all
Jon is young in years
But he knows a friend is joy and tears
His friend knows Jon as the King friend
He being the ultimate right to the end
That's why they call him a friend.

Charlie and Ronnie Kray on a boat lake in a double exposure shot.

Let's Softly Kiss

Let's softly kiss and share our bliss
Let our bodies entwine so I can call you mine
Let our hearts beat as we meet in harmony
Just you and me, Let's be one and have fun
Till our love is done

We'll be in rapture till we're spent
Let's get closer and closer
I go mad at your scent
Let's give it all we've got
We are both burning hot
Let our tongues meet and melt
You are the best I've ever felt
I like what you've got
You're the best of the lot

Let's love till the last gasp
And make it last, I'm in bliss
Let's softly kiss.

Frances on the beach in Spain.

Let's Sweat The Night Away

Just you and I in this way
Let's get close and cuddle
You put my heart in a muddle
Let's cuddle and sway
Just you and I together
And hold and kiss forever

I like your scent
It's a pleasure to pay the rent
Let our tongues meet and be one
This is real cosy fun
Lets mingle the tears of sweat
As though we first met

Let our bodies join and sway
All night and day
Lets hit the hay
Let's move as one
As your breathy gasps come fast
It will make our love last
Together we'll cling
Lets have our fling
Till the last gasp
Let's sweat the night away.

Reg with Frances.

Dreams

Your dreams are my dreams
So lets share each other while we share our dreams
Let's climb to the top of each mountain together
Let's entwine our thoughts forever
Let me be part of your desires
And let me share your smiles
Lets cross the river together

Let me get continuous joy from your laughter
It is boundless in you
I love you with every sing
Your fragrance brings you closer to me and brings you near
How fortunate I was to discover you in this vast sphere

Let's share our visions expectations
And plant our roots like a large oak tree
I love you with the power of a great ocean
In my heart there is no doubt of confusion
I love you for real
So let my kiss be my seal
Let our dreams roll together, let this be for eternity.

Reg carries Frances in Morocco.

I left My Friend Behind

I left my friend Reggie behind me
But in spirit he walks beside me
We saw much adversity together
And had a lot of fun too
One day we'll walk the physical path again too
I'm sure this will come true

We are the best of friends
And have seen many beginnings and ends
We'll make it yet on that you can bet
Our story has just begun
There are more steps to be run
We met in Parkhurst gaol
Saw some adversity had some fun
The story has just begun

We'll show them yet on that you can bet
In Parkhurst we walked two friends
Our story never ends
Reggie and I are friends.

Reggie Kray with friends.

Let That Heart Beat

Let that heart beat to the tap of your feet
Even when your heart is sad let it beat like glad
Your eyes will show just tap those toes nice and neat
Do not despair she will be there

Let that heart beat then she'll want to be near
Just tap those feet and wrap her up nice and neat
Then your lovelife will be complete

Let your heart beat with joy
You're her boy so jump with joy
Whistle from those lips and swing those hips
And tap those feet wrap her up nice and neat
Then your lovelife will be complete
Let your eyes smile and sing all the while.

Kingdom Of The Ages

The kingdom of youth is as the spring
When one is on a wing
The kingdom of middle age, as the summer
The kingdom of old age is as the winter
When one looks back with hunger
One should enter the age of all kingdoms
To see the beauty of each kingdom.

Reg, Frances and Johnny Squibb in Morocco.

Jody and Cody

Jody was the brother of Cody
They were bad men in the eyes of the law
Yet they stole to give to the poor

Jody and Cody were men of the Wild West
As bad men they were the best
They would blow up trains on the planes for the money
I thought this quite funny
And rob the banks without thanks
But someone put a price on their heads
So they had to tread carefully
And watch every tree and corner in memory
Soon they were betrayed for a price
By a skunk who was less than a handful of lice

And Jody and Cody were put in prison
But they were better off than the skunk who sold them out
He never heard his name being called by the shout
When the bullet caught him in the head
It was the last time he ever heard his name said
And Jody and Cody were remembered for feeding the poor.

Charlie Kray Snr and Violet in Benidorm with friends Christine, Ethel and Adele.

The Right Track

Things were going off the rails they kinda got off the tracks
I was biting my nails
my course had been going like a ship without sails
Or a train off the track

I had had too much drugs drink and promiscuous sex
I prayed to be put back on the track and felt like going on the attack
I had been frustrated like hell but decided to fight to the last bell
My prayer made sure I was still here and this is the story I tell
I looked the devil right in the eye and said I'll win and this is why
My prayer will get me there

Things were going off the rails they kinda got off the tracks
I was frustrated and biting my nails I was like a ship without sails
Or a train off the rails

The devil had weaved his evil web I was at a low ebb
Too much drugs drink and promiscuous sex
You could say my life was a wreck
So I decided to say a prayer
And looked the devil right in the face
And said I'll fight till the last bell

I felt like going on the attack
You'll not see me in hell
That's how I put the devil in his place
And now I'm back on the right track
And still here this story able to tell.

Reg and Frances in Morocco.

Masquerade

I understand it's a masquerade
Life's path tells me this story
I know and understand
But I say: Why should it be me?
Maybe I thought I was exempt of life's problems
Its just human nature
That we just have to say "Yes, it happened to me"
I do not know why
I'll hold you no grudge
But remember it could have been me
Holding you close tonight
But it is he
Physical or in my mind he is there
And I'm sad to say, but since that day
There are many who have taken your place
May be we have both grown up and apart
This is the way the story must end
Its just a masquerade.

Reg, Frances and Johnny Squibb in Morocco.

<u>Reach High</u>

I bargained with life for a penny
And life would pay no more
However, I begged at evening
When I counted my scanty store

For life is just an employer
He gives you what you ask
But once you have set the wages
Why, you must bear the task

I worked for a menial's hire
Only to learn, dismayed
That any wage I had asked of life
Life would have willingly paid.

Ronnie Kray eats at a dining table whilst Johnny Squibb looks on at Vallance Road.

The Blind Boy

His eyes could see no more
But he did not think he was poor
He could feel the shake of his friends' hands
And hear the music from the great bands
God was his guide; and, most of all
He still had his pride.

He always had the memory of his Mother's face
And remembered her dignity and grace
He could see no more, but the memory
Of his friends' faces he would have in store
God was his guide; and, he knew that
He would show him the way and had never lied.

Reggie Kray with Frances, Gary, Dolly Kray and some other unknown friends.

The Lifer

The years roll on by
You can see winter turn
To summer by the sky
Home seems far away
How much longer behind these walls must me stay?
I say a prayer for my fellowmen behind bars
Who gaze up at freedom and the stars
Let us waken from our sleep
And be as free as sheep
Let our hearts soar high
As high as birds in the sky
As we think of being free
As at long last the end of the long road
We can see.

Ronnie, Reggie and Violet Kray outside Vallance Road.

To A Beautiful Mother

When I look at the silver in your hair
How I wish you never in the world had a care
How I wish week after week
It was not always, Hello and Goodbye
You have made the weeks, months and years fly
You have been our rainbow
In a dark sky
We hope that one day it will be just, Hello
And never again goodbye.

So Have You

If you look for the worst in people
You can always find it
But if you look for the good points in people
You can always find that to
If not many you will find they are true
If like all men they have only a few
Christian coloured or Jew
And you will find so have you.

Violet Kray on holiday in Benidorm.

A Man

There was a man
And he was a great man
His heart could bleed
For his fellow brothers
He always had on his mind
The good being of others.

As a man
He was humble
He would stoop to stop
The beggars stumble
Or wash a sick man's feet
Or offer him
A sheaf of bread or wheat

He was a great man
He was God's plan
His name was Jesus.

Ronnie Kray and an unknown associate at the Empire State Building in
New York.

I Care What He Thinks

Does my friend think I am mad
Does he think I am bad
Does he think I am glad
When I should be sad?
Please God
Let him understand me
As clearly as he can see
The leaf of a tree
And let him know that I love him like a son
As I would like him to me
Like me he is in a cell
But if I could have a wish
From a wishing well
I would like to see him fee
With his heart full of glee.

Frances and an unknown friend aboard ship.

<u>Beyond The Stars</u>

You are beyond the stars
But I can dream
You go further away
From me like a toy boat
Sailing down a stream
But I am happy because
You are always in my dream

I think that you can
Never be mine
But I hope that you will get to
Like me in God's given time

All I want is for you to
Get to the top
Of every mountain
And have every happiness non-stop
Like a water fountain.

Reggie and Ronnie Kray on a night out with friends including Bobby Buckley (with grey suit and red tie) and 'Mad' Teddy Smith.

Murder

Murder here, Murder there
Murder fucking everywhere
Murder in the city
Murder in the town
Murder can cause bloodshed
Murder brings you down
Is there a fucking murderer
In your fucking town?

Murder here, murder there
Murder fucking everywhere
Murder in the Cotswolds
Murder in the Downs
Murder in the papers
Body bags and gowns
Murder runs the country
Murders running rife
Murder is the reaper
Coming to take your life.

Frances at the beach.

The Last Fix

Sitting alone in a dark empty room
Feeling uptight, I hope it comes soon
Shivering and trembling, biting my nails
Feeling neglected, worried and frail
Hush…I hear footsteps. A knock on the door
I fall off the bed and I crawl on the floor
I can't reach the handle, my arms are too week
The hand knocks again, I'm too ill to speak
The footsteps again, but this time they're gone
Another fix missed, another life gone.

USSR

Marching of the peoples feet
Keeping rhythm to the drummers beat
Crushing of Big Brothers eye
An outsiders simple question…Why?
The pain they've suffered is reason enough
To break a political eye is tough
It has taken time for the big figures to fall
But the bigger they are, the harder they fall
The hammer and sickle at last are no more
Victory to the people….they've won the Cold War.

Reggie and Frances Kray with 'Mad' Teddy Smith and friends on a night out.

Trains

6:30am and it's time to catch the train
Time to see the same old faces again
The train pulls in, it's right on time
The train pulls off as the church bells chime
One stop, two stop, three stop, four
'Tickets please, and get your feet on the floor.'

Mothers and their babies. Fathers and their sons
Little boys with Grandmas eating sticky buns
Then there's the princes of darkness dressed in uniformed black
Little men with problems, hiding under their hats
One stop, two stop, three stop, four
'Tickets please, and get your feet on the floor.'

Unheard announcements. Piercing screams
A siren blares, smoke and steam
Blood on the platform, blood on the train
Restrained anger, human pain
The smashing of glass….the bending of steel
All of those people have had their last meals
One stop, two stop, three stop, four
'Tickets please, and get your feet on the floor.'

6:30am and it's time to catch the train
We won't see the same old faces again
The train pulls in, it's right on time
The train pulls off as the church bells chime

Charlie Kray Snr and Violet in Benidorm.

My Life As A Worm

My life as a worm is not one to admire
There's no fun or pleasure, infact it's quite dire
No chance of promotion, non chance of a break
No thanks given, no give or take
Trapped in a groove on an old record disc
Travelling round, no sunshine, just mist
Emotions are hidden, ideas explored
No friends just acquaintances, crawl through my door

I guess I'll keep going, unable to see
Just what this pure teacher is doing to me
What's going to happen? What lies in store?
Questions unanswered, no keys for the door
Of knowledge, or hope, or salvation
All the things you need to know, were fed to you
By the system years ago. Deprived of material
Deprived of books. My life as a worm has a bleak outlook

One day I may leave my momentous life
And search for the freedom, to end all this strife
My life as a worm, is not one to admire
There's no fun or pleasure
Infact it's quite dire.

Frances at Steeple Bay.

Mark My Words

Mark my words....Mark Them Please
I am your conscience marked with disease
Sex and violence leak out from T.V
Runs like a river of evil to me
Struggles for power, fight till the end
Live and let live, earn the right to defend
Popular, faithful, father despised
Ignites a flame in your brain through your eyes
Two lovers kissing, mass murderer strikes
A radio questions likes and dislikes
Nuclear homework, the cracking of bones
The sound of a rainstorm, ransacking of homes
Elections political, animal rights
Spectator sports, and mindless fights
Fuelled by the poison from the river of doubt
Fresh from the media the evil leaks out
Mark my words....Mark Them Please
I am your conscience marked with disease.

Charlie Kray at George and Sue Dwyer's.